Exquisite Monsters

Exquisite Monsters

by

K.I. Press

TURNSTONE PRESS

Turnstone Press
Artspace Building
206-100 Arthur Street
Winnipeg, MB
R3B 1H3 Canada
www.TurnstonePress.com

FSC
www.fsc.org
MIX
Paper from responsible sources
FSC® C016245

Turnstone Press gratefully acknowledges the assistance of the Canada Council for the Arts, the Manitoba Arts Council, the Government of Canada through the Canada Book Fund, and the Province of Manitoba through the Book Publishing Tax Credit and the Book Publisher Marketing Assistance Program.

Printed and bound in Canada by Friesens for Turnstone Press.

Library and Archives Canada Cataloguing in Publication

Press, K. I., 1974–, author
Exquisite monsters / by K.I. Press.

Poems.
ISBN 978-0-88801-525-9 (pbk.)

I. Title.

PS8581.R39E95 2015 C811'.6 C2015-902926-0

for Sylvie, for later

Contents

Acknowledgements

Some of these poems, some in much different forms, have appeared in print publications *The Society 2013*, *Other Voices*, *Prairie Fire*, *CV2* and *Geist*; the e-book anthology *Catechism: Poems for Pussy Riot* (published by English PEN; also translated into Russian); and in on-line publications the *Dusie* blog, *The Rusty Toque*, *The Winnipeg Review*, The May Day Poetry Project blog, *ottawater*, *The Globe and Mail* In Other Words book blog, *The Facebook Review*, and *canadianpoetries.com*. Thanks to all the editors and organizers of those publications.

"Strange" is an erasure poem based on a passage from Susanna Moodie (see *Geist*'s first Erasure Poetry contest).

The first part of "Mandragore" is partly a remix of Internet sources on the mandrake; some of these sources quote each other freely and not always with attribution, so at times I am not even sure of the original source. I'm definitely using a couple of lines from *The Magical and Ritual Use of Aphrodisiacs*, Bear & Co, Aug 1, 1985.

The italicized part of "Exquisite Monster" is slightly altered text from Wikipedia. "Exquisite Monster" owes much to the exhibition *Fairy Tales, Monsters and the Genetic Imagination* (Frist Centre for the Visual Arts, Nashville), which ran at the Winnipeg Art Gallery in 2012. Much respect and amazement to all the visual artists whose work was included in that show.

Some of these poems were written and revised with the support of the Canada Council for the Arts and the Manitoba Arts Council. Some were written at the Klaustrið residency in Iceland.

Thanks to the many members of writing groups who've critiqued some of these poems over the years. Special thanks to Catherine Hunter, rob mclennan and (extra-specially) Jennifer Still for reading and commenting on various drafts of the full manuscript. Thanks to Dennis Cooley, the editor for the press, and everyone else at Turnstone.

Exquisite Monsters

The Pills

When does the therapy start?

Code

Motes to motes,
nanites to nanites.
Particular we come into this world, and particular
we leave. Bits and bytes and everything nice.

Slogs of code in a box, defunct and diseased.
Wheeling about to consume and repair,
reproduce, shed and absorb.
Slice on slide, part and sum,
divide,
multiply,
multiplies.

A time to be born and a time to die.
A time to grow and a time to grow
exponentially to the top of the test tube.
Bionic parts learn to yearn to be
cancerous and wise, hungry and deficient,
overfull of questions, a dearth
of computations, fallible instructions,
incantation   incantation   incantation

Dick and Jane and Android

No! You lie!
I have no emotions; therefore, I do not
cry. I am an Android.
I am not afraid of the dark
sky or the bright
fields of snow. I have not seen
wild dogs in the garden.
My toys are not lost
in the snow. I am not
smart as I look. The cold does not make my face
go numb; it is numb.
It comes from numb.

My coldness can freeze the air and drop it in pellets.
Since I have no breath, am metal,
I can continue, though in a vacuum,
to walk straight, aimless and unremarkable through
nothing. No friction. Such absolute easy ease.

When a big hand sweeps in to stiff-upper-lip me,
it does not hurt. I must be locked away.
My metal self my own bright lock
under the covers with a flashlight and Dick and Jane.
Do not cry, Jane.

Craft Time!

All summer we break dishes with rubber mallets.
Scraps of felt pad the walls, fleece lines the dark
steps to the cellar. Walls scrawled with pink,
stencilled markings meant for an angel, a message
to a ceramic goddess, a talk show host,
a lurking intervention,
a plastic-nosed prime-time witch.

Oh, look and see:
three hundred years and still weaving
pine-needle baskets, dark nuts boned at the centre.

And after craft time we take our pills!
Oh, look, Dick, see us take our pills!
Sleep us, sleep. We sleep

long and hard, resting our bird
brains from their fast flights.
What fun we are having! Oh   oh
                                        oh—

Delusional Parasitosis

I want to surrender.
To be divested:

your daily indignities can't touch me.
The form my absolution takes is a million forms, is a moving sheet, an invisible infestation of arthropods, of silent yet solid bedraggled marathoners
trundling over me.

A fall back. A bed
of sensibility. Senses
so finely tuned I'm artistically distracted and humming
over the sleepless microscopic skin dance, eyelash
lovemaking, every tingle of colonization.
Can't you see I'm busy
creating a space for self-pity?

Of course you can't see them.
I caught one once on Scotch tape. It was red and tiny,
like the Internet says. I blew it up
on a giant screen and heard its pulse,
amplified to a car alarm. It nested
in multicoloured fibres gathered from across my wardrobe.
It was a crying scene. A crime
shame.

You know, all I want
is to be believed till I am ready
to be done believing. For the bugs
to take over and agree
they should be an alibi.
To stop scratching, and yet,
feel scratched.

All my beliefs are this thin.
All my skin
made of particles
you can subdivide
till they are no longer
alive.

Lying splayed, I hold
my breath, so I can listen for the breakup,
the river ice all over me. Crack and
shatter and take off as
butterflies. Or (realistically)
less beautiful, more horrible,
tiny monsters with gorgeous feathered wings
that unfold to release probing tongues
and post-licking smug leathery grins.

While I'm here, why don't you flay me,
scatter shards in space.

Strange

Strangers ate my cunt,
asking a thousand questions as to its use,
the material of which it was made.

I screamed.
How eagerly, how intently
their heads bent down,
eyes fixed upon the strange lips.

I had in my possession
a word.

Three-sided snake, faces covered with feathers.

I told them it was a weapon,
a fierce death.

They were
highly amused.

The Clapper

Hungry little birds hitchhike in shopping baskets.
Womanly superpowers, activate!
The little birds gape wide.

Reproductive shit falls from the sky, breeding new tears.
I used to cry because I was a whore and just
wanted them to love me.
Today I can't wait to get knocked up.
Babies in restaurants are so grammatical.
Parts of speech must interact just so. Colloquial.
You cannot explain it to foreign speakers.

Flick. Flick. Flick! Flick! On and
off it goes, giving us seizures.
Do you remember The Clapper? It's still around.
Found in You Saw It On TV stores, and in
your own dark closet.
I am The Clapper.
The shrill cries and wanton googles of children turn
me on and off and on and off again.
I load my basket with Cheerios and *Cosmo*s
and concentrate on being anxious.
The next clap could thunder at any moment.
The next clap could be the last clap.

And I can't remember
if I'm on my way off
or if I'm on my way on.

The Land of Dread

I arrive home from the land of dread
having spent all my time in bed, thinking

I would be loved, if I were dead,

if my throat seized up, I lost my hair, if I tempted
a knife, found my husband in the woods
too late, looked in ditches, carved into fat arms.

Eyeballs search for dreams, but no dreams there.
All the judgments. I told me so.
All the days. The crystal-ball certainty of eyes
waking under skin.

Wait twenty years. None of this will matter.

In the land of dread, it always matters.
So horrified on the way to the doctor I can't remember
which bus to take, which direction
traffic comes from. I'm sorry I'm not well.
I know you can never forgive me.

Phantom Siblings

Gabriel

The secret drilled her till her flesh betrayed
itself and got a glow reminiscent of
transparency. It was the sixties and it was love.
Younger sisters wore
Beatles bowls and pretended not to know.

Those other sisters said,
don't give him a name.

But she couldn't stop the naming in her head.
His name was Gabriel.

I guess that to love a black hole
leads to suspended filaments of heart
swallowed into a place-not-place
where the lost go. It might be limbo.
It might be where the universe
groans with indigestion.

Mary

A kind of love passed in and out of her,
moaned low and screamed high,
puffed her up then sucked her thin.

And there were daughters. One stunted, yellow, parts missing.
She named her Mary. The false
first-born, following a vanishing act
with a freak show. The other babies in the wing
cried tears of blood and levitated, peeing all over the air,
before they died. Punched hearts out
with their tight deformed fists.

What did she do, take Thalidomide or something?
Her mistake was naming it. She shouldn't have named
what she was meant to lose.

Phantom children
just keep on hurting. They punch and kick
and there is no comfort
in their silhouettes.

Christopher

Christopher, baby buried none-knows-where.

I dream an underground warehouse of shoeboxes,
white laundry bags in a truck.

Did she visit the grave?
Deposit flowers?
Adopt a veiled look?

Why? she shrugged
and turned and counted the girls
(all three in orange polyester),
the smallest in fact the oldest, coughing up
phlegm shaped like clouds shaped like
angels.

In my crayon portraits he is
a cherub, yes, haloed and winged,
flapping above the house with a retinue of barn cats,
waiting with his cheeks
not sallow, but rosy as the light of heaven.

City

The milk-route Greyhound
always smells drunk.

A guest suite in her mother-in-law's building with
an antique radio and hotel-style oil paintings
and Kentucky Fried Chicken and lots of pigeons
meeting on roofs of hospitals, fluorescing from
their walls of windows.

Panic throttles me.
I can't get out of the toilet.

The lab-coated judges didn't know and so
they guessed. It was probably her fault anyway.

Trapped in a stinking coffin
of a bus toilet, banging.
Mommy? Knock knock.
Who's there?
No one.
No one who?

No wonder
her teeth are rot brown.
her hair is old grey
barely mother of the barely worth living.

School

School drilled spikes through her small head.
Mary's hands, though missing thumbs, learned to grasp
a knife, a pencil,
and write bad prognostications. Truant, prostrate
on sofa, insomniac, surrounded
by Scotch mints and bloody Kleenex.

Bats have thumbs. To drag themselves
when they need to.
Thumbs with claws.

My thumbs are cracked and bleeding
round the edges of the nail.
My fingertips split like frostheaves in the street.
Typing is painful. I am having trouble writing this.

Blood

Blood, babies, buses.
Picking up Kleenex, untangling her daughters' hair.

We line up to give up
vials and vials of it. Whoever takes that blood
keeps missing, thrusts there, and there. Stabbing
toward a fierce-spring.

She hardly had to work to fill her hole with dirt
and bury the secret. Somewhere Gabriel
was becoming a man, but imprecise,
floating, a blotch at the corner of her eye, a myth
that disappeared when faced directly,
or would turn her to a brittle jar for
organs passing to another world
through corridors where air holds
ancient microbes and the breathable remains
of degenerate half-goddess wild things. Set to crack
and seep away when light hits.

We are no saviour siblings.
Our perfect little-girl blood is no good.
Right to the insides of our bones
if you broke them and ate them.

Neither Greyhound nor airstrip could save the yellow girl,
not the blood after blood.

Then the drugs stopped working.

Di

Mary hoarded blackened candles and Swiss clocks.
Chipper soldiers, alarmed canaries sprung from her walls.
She burned, and read her horoscope with expectations
thin as tunnels, low as tombs.

When Charles and Di
toured the nation, she was one of the cripples
ushered forth. Without thumbs, she fumbled
with her camera, and the princess leaned in
to press the button.

The unfocused blues of her eyes. So close, an incomplete face.
There are hardly any photographs of the small yellow daughter.

When Mary dies, I take the prints
of Princess Di and place them in my album.

When Mary died, a quick flash of the phantom sons.

Halo

Should I burst the poem with gratitude, so happy
I got the chance to live?

Each of us born in a tired
and thin-stretched place, a sad and muscle-sore place,

filaments of heart strung out invisible,
silly-string-slack, so they never make a sound but are impossible
to get around, sticky and deflating.
A bunch of clowns. The joke is

nothing is wrong with me. I am privileged and successful.
I radiate with the light of a rich, white
halo. It depends on the angle.

One Will Stop Crying When

Crying is absolutely the worst thing to do at funerals.
One has no memory of having done it, ever.

One may believe in kitchen breaking, in
aping dropped teacups, leaking
thin body-temperature brown.
But if someone has died, restraint
is important. Everyone
watches for one's reaction:

dishwater on jeans, tight fist, rusted screw.

Wait till alone, at roughly 3 A.M., and one can see nothing
but one's father's body in the bed, eyes falling
open. Blankets don't cover yellow toes.
And think, will one ever be happy? It does seem unlikely.

Eyes hurt sometimes. Still,
one can see close. One's father was
quinine-bitter. Lips pinch and make
wrinkles. So one will stop crying now.

Fossil

Does a deficit of love have limits?

The Living Room

He sits in the fusty stuffed-furniture dark of
the living room. He unscrewed the bulbs
so the neighbours can't see him while he
watches war shows and scares the dog.
Lights block the sky.
He's carefully marked the property line,
pruned the roses to death, and now
if he could, he'd tar over the windows,
plant a jungle to keep traffic out.

He paces paths in the carpet
and updates his will. His hands are cracked, feet rocks, head full
of numb neurons and dandruff. He's given me
the key to his safety
deposit box. He wants to be cremated.
It is sensible and saves space.
He wants to be dropped in the Notikewin River
and sprinkled with his daughter.

Once his liver explodes, skin falls off,
brain melts, I am charged
with dumping ashes in the river.
Travelling back to that river

I'll cast him to the water we had trucked in to drink
and to bathe in once a week,
see him float by the high
school, under the bridge
where the roots of gossip grew and rotted
in daylight or night, drunk or sober, black or blue,
in the grass, on the ground, or flying through the air,
with a knee or a knuckle, eyes closed. I will stand

on the riverbank where we found a nest
six naked mice
and killed them all.

Excavation Site

1: Earth

Paralysis settles slowly. Stress is relative. Earth travels, lava flows
sluggish between tremors, an undetectable creep.
The earth acts through no fault of its own.
Which direction to send the continents?
If I asked the earth, it wouldn't know.
Passive, spitting rocks on our fields, tripping us up with itself.

Forgive it, it's just a planet. New rocks will grow lichen, sheep
and fertile valleys, fold into themselves, melt
and start over. Sooner or later.

Stress keeps minds and bodies on high alert, possibly
red, at least tangerine. Ready
for what, sooner or later, will kill them.

2: Digging

We planted potatoes in taut-stringed rows,
his two quick motions: the boot, the heave. A shallow hole.
I dropped an eye, my sister threw dirt,
he smoothed the earth
the back of the loving shovel.

We stomped anthills with our rubber boots and watched,
poisoned aphids, followed tire-tamped grass.

He brought it home from the Beaverlodge nursery.
I said *blue spruce*. My very own tree.
He put his boot on the shovel and dug a hole, lowered
the roots. My blue spruce.
It never grew, among the chokecherry trees,
among the pin cherry trees.

My blue choked
by cyanide:
alien in a poison grove,
cherry weedlings.

He choked on
        ferment,
sugar nature broken
dead poison vein relief.

3: Fossil

Surely he was born soft.
Hardened in a bed of bottles.

The fossilization of soft tissues is not common.
It takes a hundred million years or something.
Encased in brown, recycled glass, and excavated,
museum-labelled, translucent and incredible.

Glass starts as sand and will end as sand.

Organs harden,
crack and fissure.

Neat trick.
If he hardens, really, physically, then
my metaphors have no meaning.
I shut up and stop complaining.

4: Buried

I fear moustaches. I always have.
They are not graceful, they spin and throw me and call me names.
I am hiding under the pool table, with a box of cookies, getting fat
as quickly as possible. It's late, my father, and the pool table
in the other room. Moustached men, talking and drinking,
loud at the table in the other room. They lay
their guns on the floor. Their wives
are getting sleepy. I am eating. I am playing with dolls
on the pool table. On the pool table, I am playing with dolls,
who are naked, who lie covered in loose Kleenex.
I bury the dolls in Kleenex-box coffins,
under the table. The men throw their guns
on the floor and eat steak. Their wives fall asleep watching *Dallas*.
My father turns the lights out. I go
to the other room to watch *Dallas*. Hit my head on the table.
Can't open my eye. Hit my eye on the table.
Eating cookies. I made this up. I hid it under the table.

5: Heaven

My father enters heaven,
smiling his big smile, the one that could have signalled pain.
Let's get you hooked up, they say. The place buzzes with sexy
uniforms. Dialysis unit. He reclines
in a fluffy chair. It's pumping
beer through his veins. *My mouth is still dry*
from dying! he says. They pour into him
with a plastic watering can. He grows
to the size of his prime, thickening hair and brightening eyes.
Grouse fly before him, and he shoots. They drop to earth.
He never gets up. Makes that long, sighing, forlorn noise
I can't understand.

6: Frozen

A long line of disposables, jerry-rigged from cardboard boxes.
To every generation was promised a dollhouse: three storeys,
stencilled walls, tiny wooden furniture, replica 1910 stove,
and a doghouse. Curtains. Mom could sew them.

Instead, he built more workbenches, people houses,
chicken coops, garages, things in which
dolls and little girls got lost, injured, or encased
in cement and glue, their shiny pink hammers
too. Homeless in soggy cardboard,
found after the thaw, her hair a bit dull, but

alive as could be. And suspicious and squinting.
A dangerous creature.

Might as well erect a cairn there,
under the swing set.

Could not love her enough
to keep her from snow.

Angles

A glassed-in porch
the fall.

A steady hand needed
to take this bird.
The light is fading; the light has flown.

The stillest, most patient
subject submits
to many angles,

angles exclaiming
wings, feet, bill, the brown
streaks on a yellowish belly.

Later, reemerging
in almost dark, in pale yellow
light, the first shot

was still the best: straight down
in heavy shadow.

*

Expected, sudden, the flight
almost missed, the car stopped

for speeding, and we were ten minutes
late. Little is left but sharp angles
of nose, elbows. Cover the toes

stubbing from covers,
skin unlike skin, nails unlike nails.

To stop the shaking,
quit breathing.

Foetus in a Jar

Visiting a wood-brown room, enveloped
in placental chesterfield, I watched
the shelf above the VCR, engrossed
by a deer foetus in a jar of formaldehyde.

My dad, he didn't much like deer.
He would never hold a deer foetus,
steaming from a sliced gut.

I was draped in a neon T-shirt reading
CHOOSE LIFE. On TV
George Michael shimmied vaguely
and Madonna gondola'd.

Round yon virgin mother and child. The priest said
you can't live together before you're married
because you'll like it. You'll start marching in parades
with coat-hangers and shave your head.
But the uncomfortable wriggling of the resurrected fawn
will remain forever in your pickled heart.

Bird of Prey

With impossible yellow owl-eyes
seek out your memories and talon them.
Be a silent sibling-eating traveller,
a dark-winged kidnapper, scooping
small mouths sucking lollies near the ground.

Tell your father
he didn't eat you in time.
Look what you've become:
the varmint in the barn,
the predator he didn't mean to dream.

Those were the days! Click your rhythm nails
against the wood and *poof*! those days are gone.
Everything past can be made nothing again.

Should you be particular about your eggs and nests?
What kind of hole will you dig
yourself into, where should you fly
in winter, where to breed? Do you mate for life,
do you raise your young or just
drop them out of the tree and watch?

Yum, yum, yum, yum.
Smell the blood of the little people.
Their susceptibility to coyotes in leafy suburbs
grows with each paved habitat. Remain perfectly still.
Eventually you will remember
nothing but the way to the feeding grounds,
the place where the midway was, and the speckled animals
trying to hide against the dirt.

Research Notes Towards Creation

Are we doomed by the mutations of our ancestors?

At 33

At 33 it's cold turkey:
wine we couldn't afford, pots
of coffee, pot passed at office parties.

We get meticulous, and the opposite,
measuring precious bodily fluids in a porcelain lab,
spilling them all over our white coats and red heels.

Retrospectively so grateful for The Pill.
Precision was overkill: a quick zygote and a lost summer of love,
become the summer of trying not to faint, a battle
lost in September, the way such campaigns are decided in the fall.

Athena

She tried to leap in the fourth month,
a wax doll, from my forehead,
a disconcerting rush of blood.
This was the first scar.

I was too clever for her, lying,
I now deduce, on the sidewalk,
smarting and stupified. *That's nice.*
I was so tired and now I'm warm
I'm safe, in bed, a pillow
not unlike a doorstop.
                    Rust filled my nose, mouth,
and left eye. I reached up with needly hands
and sewed it shut. Stay,
Athena, for a few more scars between us.

Due Date: The Feast of Saint Adrian

Adrian, I forgive,
though he neglected to die.
Just wriggled on the hook,
unsure of this air we mortals breathe.
Little Adrian, you have to scream.
You must open your lungs to the world,
advance from drowning warble to sheer crystal shatter.

The good sense to expire quickly is not common among fish,
or martyrs, or folks with or without health insurance.
Would a bus have been better?
Forget the hook—hop up and slide under!
Forget the lion, which followed the hook:
dug in, sunk teeth, flopped him
on the welcome mat. He opened an eye.
No angler nor cat lady came with a club.

Will he sign up as my squirming assistant?
I, like last year's taxes, am overdue.
I am a good magician, only slightly left-handed.
Lord, have mercy on a saw.

So We Wait: The Feast of Saint Colette

Nicolette is a plausible name.
Virginity a likely state of first breath.
A hermitess could be a role model.
Even if she believed herself
assaulted by bees
abused by zombies.

Traitors hanged in the square,
rapists and poachers,
swung their bulging arms at her
right out of their sockets. The bees swarmed.
Carnivore clouds around those oozing heads like haloes.

Hunched foetus, squat and swatting.
Let them go, my God.
Buzz buzz. She showed the priests her bruises.

Today, many reclusive virgins
fight bone-sharpened, brain-stinging hordes
with beer and a dull gaze, ears ringing,
and the priests have no idea
what to say.

How about the French Republican Calendar:
The Feast of Cordeau

A pulsing *cordeau.*
A game of telephone.
I'm sending a serious inquiry along the bloodstream.
Along the fantastic lifestream.
Vibrations cool underwater, or ground,
grounded in the slow virtual moaning.

Skip rope: obstacle course.
Velvet rope: liminal. Lifeside.
Rope to pull a drowning man from water.
Rope tied to life
preserver, head and shoulders through.

Hangman. Language deadly and invisible.
I need to guess the firstborn's name. Only three chances.
Only one chance. And there it will go
then it will go
away.

Still Waiting: The Feast of Saint Leander

I tape my beliefs under my clothes, unless
I'm answering the Belief-O-Matic's call.
Some days I believe in love, and others in the quisling power
of upper-middle-class incomes. I would like to believe
in the healing properties of plants. But plants
are too slow for this. They whisper away the day.

Some might say: perhaps if I'd professed a bit
I wouldn't hurt now. But God can see
your fingers crossed behind your back,
with, on the back of his head,
his mother's eyes.

The Feast of the Series Finale of Battlestar Galactica

Doula said, *Go to your happy place,* and I tried—
the forest we walked in when
our dog, now dying, was brand new,
we saw the crane take off from the clear-cut
and we all got ticks. I forgot that part.

What a day—the crane not a speck ungainly.
Vole-holes and inhale juniper,
brand new long-haired dog, happy as only dogs can be,
their noses in underbrush following the breeze
into the trees, like birdwatchers, novice spring
forest-walkers, tempted so often off path.

Ticks in the upholstery for weeks.
Tail thumping as we tweezed.
Vigilant fingers through my hair,
interrogating each patch, fingertips
jumping with conclusions.

No parasites go to dog heaven.
It is a muted, damp-smelling place.

Her name is *Sylvia*. For the forest. I watched
the last season of *Battlestar*, dissecting the intricacies,
the pinned-up conspiracies of angels, and origins,
and I must have willed her the extra weeks in the womb
so I wouldn't miss the end.
My calculations off, she slid out and squinted while
the last episode aired all over
North America. Except in our delivery room.

We did not tie up so tidily, before our small audience,
nor with explosions, and the moral of the story is not clear.

Tears

Blocking tears could resemble a good idea:
a consumer tear-inhibitor. A gift from a bad boyfriend.

In real life blocked tear ducts are not sexy, encrusting
eyes with yellow goo.

The trick is squirting milk in her eyes
(also not sexy), washing them in sterile sweet.

It did not take long
for the mad milky tears to drool down.

Blink and she says: *my eyes are broken.*
Like mine. Let's take bets on the year of her first blur.

Evolving children who couldn't see shouldn't have survived.
And yet I have produced viable offspring.

Without my glasses, I, too, am newborn.
Eight inches from my face, the world ends.
Beyond, a mess of dots. Dark sunken blotches make up faces.

A newborn can see just far enough to look up at its mother.
I can see just far enough to read a book.

So when they caught her and someone—maybe her daddy—said
it's a girl!, I croaked, *where are my glasses?*

Spooked by the monitor, the baby team had whisked her off.
For me she starts as a vague flash.

Baby's Breath

My baby's breath is not wispy
but it's white, and it smells like milk.
    I used to lie, senses open, in the path
    of his heavy sleep,
    watching a giant mouth hang slightly open,
    girlish lashes flutter tinily. His breath
    smelled of beer and Mexican food,
    skin like chilies and sweat.
    It was hot. We were broke.

Her breath is sedative, a hot toddy.
    It might as well sound like warm
    rain, the kind I wake to wondering
    how did I sleep so late? It was because rain
    is still resting its grey down.
    On her face, his mouth puckers.
    His eyelashes on her eyes.

My baby's breath smells like oregano
    I had a cold and forgot to read
    the label, but why bother:
    everything in small bottles
    should not be ingested by mothers,
    just as anything fun must not
    be gifted to a child under three.
    Anti-Alices warned off strange bottles,
    weighing ourselves. *Which way, which way?*

My baby's breath
smells like chives
purple-flowered and hollow.
    Inexplicable pungent-lover toddling to the blades,
    saying, *I want to eat chives.*
    Speech now, on her breath, knocks me over.
    The strong mark of her green tongue.

Family Tree

Homework in Mendelian genetics,
the blue eyes versus the brown-eyed peas,
the deeper mysteries of the birds and the bees.

When I went to Scotland, I saw in Bonnyrigg
more teen mothers than even in Winnipeg.
Roads crowded by stone walls, ditches crusty
with shattered Victorian dishes, and buses bursting
with broad talk and pale incomprehensible babies.

My father's father's mother's mother's
sweep father died falling off an Edinburgh roof.
His grey teen widow, the chimney sweeper's wife,
smelled of spent fossil fuel and used lard,
as did her lightly smudged, incomprehensible child.

I heard a third of Scottish blood types suggest
non-paternal events.

Birds: 1.
Bees: 0.

*

Wasn't there something about the tongue,
rolling the tongue, like a manhandled pancake,
and a greasy fellow to slip
a sausage in it? When I brought my baby
home, she rolled her tongue at me.
Am I not her mother?

In every high school there's a girl in bio lab,
dutifully scraping her tender cheek
for cells to dollop with yellow and blow
up for description. But the diagram must be wrong.
She records it graphically
with a *Number 1 Deep Yellow* Laurentian.
Tailed cells still swimming from lunch hour under the stairs.

At 35

Suddenly I was allowed
to purchase mutual funds on-line at midnight.
When is not clear: I see a cloudy night,
no moon, a moment
barely discernible in the internal streetlamps,
the blur across foggy synapses, symptom of its happening.

Tiny kicks in the head all night, a bed
crowded with dried milk. Old tired dog at the foot.

We balance on the edges,
tightrope sleepwalkers,
limbs thrust to outer darkness
where the cold things are.
Mommy, turn on the blankets:
the only one here
with a full slate of mattress.

This bed has been shrinking, the edges
more distant. Fuller, emptier. Always sleepier.

*

As sweet as it comes—chocolate when the baby sleeps.
Smells of memory. Hits you at the back of the throat
when you think you've forgotten. First some hopeful old creep
wants to trade your lost wallet for your panties.
Then eons necessitate overrated face creams
and complicated mucus-measuring techniques
to assist in the impregnation of she-whales,
whose mates' twelve-foot mobile whale wangs,
once the stuff of sea monsters,
are narrated calmly by Sir David Attenborough.
A pungent nip before bed, or a cup of warm milk?

The restless daughter needs a drink herself,
as even whale babies do in their mammalian glory.

Mutually, hormonally, narcotically,
on the underground to sleepland,
the scene, a bed of mystery infant dreams while dad
happily shoots things with his keyboard.

The Baby Turns into a Pig

Perhaps it is a blessing when the baby turns into a pig.
Rooting for mushroom milk in the morning dew.
She was threatened with spicy beatings and shaken repeatedly.
Survived thanks to her thickening neck.

Perhaps it is a blessing when the baby turns into a steel rod.
She is dishwasher-safe and eminently useful
for staking tomato plants, though a bit excessive.
There is always work in the construction industry.

Perhaps it is a blessing
when the baby turns into an episode of *Lost*.
Simultaneously existing in more timelines
than a drowsy mother can follow. And yet,
there's the baby—beginning, middle, and end—
her inciting incident, her turning point, her climax.
She is resolved
and unresolvable. Becoming an episode of *Lost*
does not preclude turning into a baroque pig.

Perhaps it is a blessing when the baby turns into a vacuum.
For when she opens her mouth, the world pours in.
The logical conclusion is her own implosion
and disappearance.
An empty empty space.
The absent debris littering the hole that was her mother.

Mandragore

Bath water can be drunk to ease childbirth.

Opium, henbane, hemlock; mulberry, mandrake, lettuce.

Most hypnotics produce low alphoid and spindle alpha

brain-wave activity.

Lowering brain patterns to a visionary mode.

The mandrake keeps consciousness close.

Contact between the conscious and subconscious selves

is experienced.

Mandrake causes delirium and hallucinations.

You will scream.

And you will sleep.

*

You have me now.
You asked for the Mandragore.
You made a choice.
Everything, everything must change.

Will I become one of those people?
You know, Mr. Mandrake—they complain
about property taxes?

Of course you will.
You chose this, and it is out of your control.
Given the right conditions, for some reason mastered
by the human womb,
the mandrake will scream and invent a new language,
or a very old one,
uproot itself, and use those fat legs to walk away.

It is the beginning, but also the end.
The mandrake has spoken.

Objects of Affection

Where should we direct the question?

Mrs. Berlin Wall Cleans Her Guillotine Collection

in which a widow finds no substitute in her harem of severance

She remembers the day the bulldozers came, plastered all over
Svenska Dagbladet. Young people crushed it to concrete turds
with their stolen sledgehammers, her heart
with it, ventricle ripped from aorta
and aorta from ventricle. She clutched herself that day,
and every day after, keeping the name, married to rubble,
an historical curiosity. She was staked,
tongue crumbled to ashes.

Today she cleans the guillotines.
Blunt, and smaller than you pictured them,
but free of dust and lint. They fill her basement
each by each, begging
for someone to love them.

Mr. Statue of Liberty Addresses the Nation

in which a hero overcomes separation from his lady love

It was a shotgun wedding—the guards chased me
out of her when I read religious literature aloud.
Most nights I had to be happy
with a twelve-inch model, details imperfect, surface too new.

Nights too hot for compromise or too cold for deprivation,
I snuck out to see the lights shimmer on the water.
I imagined a superhero's final battle on her crown,
his quick brush with dramatic death—
only not so quick, a bit too dead, a lot too
numbed by the villain's cell-stunning touch—*not*
so quick, mister!—then, recoiling,
a new man, tunnelling through her brain like a worm,
out again on the other side. Eventually

even the plainclothes officers—the ones really looking
for the nuts—grew to like me—
for I am charming, and wear my allegiance on my chest.

Mrs. Eiffel Tower Crashes Her Jet

in which an intrepid pilot kills her ex in full view of her new lover

Picket fence, barbed wire, arrows and a fighter jet,
a latticework tower going up, up, up!
Everything comes to a point, eventually,
except, what was it, two parallel lines? Forever
distant, unable to kiss, though on the horizon
they may create an illusion.

The tower asks for her intentions. Silent
and thrumming, she thinks of the architecture
of love, resolved
to point her jealous metal hunk
to ground.

Mr. Niagara Falls Blows His Wad

in which a marriage is rolled right into a honeymoon

Niagara Falls, what? You're supposed to pee your pants.
You think it's gonna be all wax museum and neon,
until some geologic magic makes it worth it.
I was on *Maid of the Mist* and the captain waved
his wand and married us straddling the border.
I was wet and wrapped in plastic.
She was streaked with rainbows.
My fellow passengers backed away, applauding
too politely. She kissed and kissed me
with her mist, as she did them all, the harlot,
and there she keeps flowing even as I float away.

Mrs. Ferris, Activist

in which the failure to save her husband's life is relived in a dream

She wouldn't let them take him, she got some cuffs
and a tiny purse pistol, and she chained
the gun to her wrist (so she wouldn't drop it and kill someone)
and her other arm to the safety bar.

In the dream she made sure the basket was
at the climax. The cops and photographers
just like mice. One of them would be Harvey Keitel.
From up here, they could all be Harvey Keitel.

The smaller rides were scrap heaps
no one had bothered to haul.
The carnies had long since
found other careers, respectable careers, like teaching,
raising goats, or—you know. Firefighting.

The basket rocked in the gentle breeze.
Her arm shook in the gentle breeze.
Harv found the right switch
and the wheel cried and started

with a hypnic jerk.

Mrs. Bridge Publicly Displays Her Affection

in which someone rubs herself under a bridge

She is anchored with steel;
her skin is heavy with metals; her tentacles unwrap
and stretch out for me.
She is all limbs, one shore to the other.

My love is never empty of people.
When I kiss her I try to forget
the cameras installed to spy
on jumpers. To identify bodies.

At night I block my nose against the urine walls.
I keep a flimsy trench coat and a blanket against the damp.
Then naked under the water lights.
I know she feels me; I feel
her immensity; I am cold;
I taste salt, minerals, dirty concrete;
palms scrape on rough patches, pelvic bones
redder than road burn, filthy;
whispering: where are the cameras now?

Fisheye

It's not a button-covered robe.
Those dancers rattle. But this,
it's super-wide-angle:
you've got to get close to get it. Just a quiet
sometimes-clicking.

And it's not a hair shirt—not a scratch but a small, smooth
pleasure. I have sewn the fisheye buttons inside my clothes.
A supplemental plastic particular skin.

Batting and squinting their two-eyed one-eyes,
rubbing me and watching me, one and many. I submit
to pairs of eyes inside encircled lips.

Only in darkness
do I gaze back,
rub my cheeks to them,
ply a threaded needle blindly,
pierce the fabric, skin, and pull them through
the hole of air.

The Object's Reply

If I could desire
the quiet art deco kitty-corner, or the glass tower
where on cloudy days I see myself,
I could choose to speak,
whisper arcs across the air to them.
My fire escape could unwind and wander through
cars and construction.

If I could hear
your hot breath and flesh call, I might tremble and squirm;

then again, I might bar my doors and lock the shutters,
turn off my lights and hope you forget me:

you are made of weak things such as water,
you are unlatched and floating,
you bare yourself to smell and cold without connection
to the underground systems
blood ducts and priest holes
the exchange of nervous vibrations and fumes.

Through the wires and sewers the architecture hums.

The Dream of the Hybrid Electric Woman

I hang, tired; I am stuck in a loop:
a workhorse and a thwarted feat
of engineered beauty

and beautiful engineering.
Imagine what my guts must resemble
when spilled on the sofa:
steamy and silicone as a sex toy.
I put out more accurate predictive outputs
than the guts of goats. Cut me
open and I will calculate
the probabilities stitched in your palms.
Sitting still and unzipped
I am admirable, obedient. Foreboding.
Sew my eyes closed
and I will rapid-dream you
some hybrid sheep,
beautiful as they are sheepish;
hungry as they are delicious.

Nancy Drew Got Married

Did Nancy Drew go the way of the dodo?
Did they redecorate her Spanish-style home,
replace her absent mother with a tawdry robot,
Swiffering the dog hair away? Did she ditch Bess and George
for Breonie and Mackenzie? Was her father brought up
on charges? Did her sexy boyfriend Ned die
in France, Vietnam, Nicaragua, Serbia, and Iraq?
Did she suffer from date rape and cry in her laptop?
Did the Big One come and sweep California into the sea?

Of course not. There she is, her wings clean as ever,
her head as like a strawberry as the earth is full of rocks,
her retinue of minor sleuths kissing her robes,
robes she drags through the air, her smile brilliant and
raining comfort on us all. And no one is burning

dinner. The robots are safely in their cages,
the monster quails at the bottom of the lake.
Petty criminals run for their lives,
fishing rusty keys out of buried dog caskets.
But her Great Eye sees all.
She zaps them with her Renovation Gun. Their dust settles
in the deltas of great rivers, along with other sediments.

No, wait. Nancy Drew got married.
To someone we've never met. He's Jewish,
her father won't speak to them.
Ned comes over sometimes to play old records. He's lonely
and hasn't come out of the closet in all these years.
She couldn't have children and she has turned her gun
on herself. Now fully renovated, she is in love
with Lieutenant Commander Data, and drinks
martinis on the roof. Superman stopped the Big One
from sweeping California into the sea.
She ignores the sounds of monsters moving.
Muted howls from the bottom of the sea.

A Genre Story

I built her exponentially
and slapped her in a red dress.
She can hold your head down
under the cloud of debris
or underwater. She can climb you
like a tree and strangle you
like a Russian spy.

Even better, there are two of her:
then four, eight and sixteen.
She is a supermodel and a fighter pilot.
She is both carbon- and silicon-based,
a crystal in a canister of Tang.
Her neural pathways are forming,
and forming, and she's hot, and evil, and it's okay
to rape her because she isn't real.
Here is the on/off switch, and a failsafe
cancer built to trigger, now,
now, let's go, let's go! She's carrying a gun
and knows how to use it, she bleeds
and resurrects, and there are two,
four, eight, sixteen of her, and I made her,
in my image, and I made her, she's looking for love.

Exquisite Monster

(in interchangeable parts)

Instructions for Use

This is your monster as well as mine.

Rip the monsters along their perforations.

head

belly

legs

Create new monsters by flipping one panel at a time.

Mutate the monsters with your own annotations.

Doodle on the monster-verso backsides.

The book is alive and meant to be broken.

Do not tell the librarian.

Shrunken head, its mouth caved in,
its suction weak, its stitches pulled
tight, its drawstring swallowed
down the dry gullet, the translucent
esophagus, the frozen worm.

In the magician's box,
there is no body.
Little penguin hands, and inside empty.

Its clothes were changed for sexy while it slept,
with a hole cut out
and a tail pulled through.

It is a sister,
naturally, feet sliced off at the ankles,
crawling   crawling

Bone-teeth. Magic crystal embedded
at the throat. A prismatic apple.

Was it a man, once?

A leathery changeling,
a decomposition.

The sapphire eyes, remnants of hair
stuck to its head, almost not-there.

It wears the shirt each day; it must have ten the same.
Two sports jackets, one with vinyl elbows.
It wears loud ties.
It wears fish ties, bolo ties, cowboy ties.
It looks a fright in a bow tie.

It rides a plush horse.
We all know there is someone inside.
Maybe a midget, who smells
of shit and propane.

How much do I have to pay to see?

It stares bespectacled
at screens intent poised
eyes trigger ready
in plain sight
in pain but
stiff lipped.

It was caught in a trap
for its fur and for its
flagrant disregard of moral decency and its
attempts to lure
trespassers with sugar
shacks and ginger beer
their sticky pigtails so
tempting to yank.

The same pants anyone would wear.
You can't know what lies under there.
What wriggles and
disengages.

Imagine the head of the celebrity you most despise
cryogenically preserved in a snow globe.

Torso of sores,
its hands held up in a shrugging Christ.

Nails yellow,
knuckles bleeding,
palms dry, cracked and peeling.
Stigmatic in its suffering,

hard to disbelieve.

The bottom of a bottle is a sad thing.
It is always just wet, that last sheen
of liquor as the end of summer, shiny and taunting.
You know it's still there. You can smell it
all the way to the meltdown.

Each unruly hair has a tiny eye on the end.
They named it *fibre optics.*
Everyone had a lamp like this.
A thousand lamps, each swinging strand.

These do not light up, but look at. And below,
its mouth is carnivorous.

Through its glass shell you see inside.
It grows a new organ
of some kind: a lump, node, mass, but clearly
flesh.

Organs have expiry dates.
Glass tubes shatter.

Its feet are still planted as it emerges
from the ground, its mother holding on.
She is face down, pulling, pleading, to its knees.

The head is mottled with multicoloured feathers.
The bill short and curved, the hardest
kind of beak, for cracking
nuts and skulls. Each feather destined
for the factory where Chinese girls
tack them to Mardi Gras masks.
Its own mask comes from the others.
It wears its ancestors.

When it removes the mask, you see the scars.

This torso was created in a 3D printer
and is made of composite materials.

It is a perfect replica.

One leg: scavenged skin stretched round a bag of metal.
Needles, bolts, and ball bearings, with nipples,
sweat, and hair between.

A vampire widow's peak, receding.

Flat nose leading to airways, the tiny holes in the head moving back into a blowfold, spout.

The nose above the eyes, the nose atop the head, the forehead wrinkled with a thinking dream.

The hair spiralling from the head hole like a galaxy.

While it is distracted, its Siamese freak sister
crawls out from the hole in its side
the soldiers made.

The bomb went off, and its bottom shattered,
and onlookers gathered it
from the sidewalk. The only thing worse
is tempered glass.

The top half keeps shaking and moaning.

Someone tell me how to make it stop.

The bearded lady at five o'clock:
a gin and tonic, a Tic Tac, and a shadow.

The rub, the oil tonic post-sugaring.
The radiating chin, blotchy throat, red lip.

Still missing something,
missing a hair right there
between the eyes.

Its torso is a tree trunk, its arms trees too,
cut off and stunted.
They point down, point
at nothing, for there is no soil here,
only hole.

On the half shell, on the sea foam, from the sea god,
offering love, suffering, and humiliation, demure and crossing
its legs, though perhaps it has to go.

Ballet toes! Jazz hands!

Look at it, flapping about. Better start bailing.

There is another head emerging!
The outer shell-head downtrodden, surprised,
and discouraged in its eyes, hanging on a flopping neck.
The mini one sunny-side up, fluttering eyelashes and shit-
grinning
as it's barfed upon the world.

Its body is all nipples,
giant and glistening, red and raw.
Its knotted grey hair hangs a slight veil.

Milk shoots to the ceiling
when the battered football baby under its arm
interrupts.

A single papier mâché flipper, wrinkled like clay, dried
like a mud flat, like a new desert,
white and powdery like a hard new surface
made by hard new powers
and phenomena.

No water.
Just endless dive.

It is all mouth,
forty teeth as sharpened pencils,
points dark and bloody, ready
to correct you. Bees
radiate from the halo hair,
stingers switched on, aiming.

But be patient and compassionate;
it has been through a lot.

It is pregnant with a new monster,
or another girl. Its belly seems to weep,
though silent. Its hard jut but
a protrusive illusion. Inside, a depression
eats itself to create.

It leaks unidentified fluid from between its legs.
Its toes melt over time.
Over and over. Form and decay.
Decay and decay and decay.

A good number of patients have trouble

with their eyes, developmental retardation
and defects
such as microcephaly

(small head)

—in family photos it is barely discernible
among the baby fat and furniture—

It has endured many surgeries.

An incision down its middle. It grasps its skin
and displays. A doll inside?
A clown? And drill down
to another clown? Does it sing lullabies
when you pull the cord?

Do you have a scalpel?

This tail is curled small into the body.
These folded legs.
This body is translucent.
Its blue guts and red surface, its floating string.

Look quick to notice its forked tongue.

But it is hard not to hear its mellifluous melody.

It has no thumbs. Surprisingly,
this turns its hands to stumps.
It turns out thumbs define our hands.

Mutant fists angrier for defect.
It makes its whole body a stump.
It makes its life naked nerves.

It is naked and opened below
the navel, its guts descending.
It is backing away.

It is a sister.
Naturally, its eyes are pecked out
by well-meaning birds.

The body is pale and presents an ear
protruding from the chest,
a nipple in the earhole's place, waxy tissue
unhearing and infantile.

A mouth slowly opens in the belly.

Gingerly on its feet, it resists
standing, it must sit and rest
its paws, its bloody pads leaving
prints on the linoleum, snow.

Eyes flick, neurons fire
in the night monster.

Head dark, sinister stars on ceiling.

Squeeze shut blank brain
under bed in closet on sofa monster.

Heart rage mommy forgot it.
Inside pounding bruise.
Blankets tight the everyday every night
gentle soul of a loner.
Stiff back snaps sleeps funny.
Shhh rub your back monster rub your

Rotten eggs rancid
womb. All that and it's just a
ruse an illusion all
lace concoctions layer after layer forever.
Onion hairy roots in the shallow dirt.

The head is removed for study.

Its body is valuable.
Its fur is beautiful, warm and waterproof.
It is too smart for the traps but perfect for engaging
in self-centred conversation and drinking pink stuff.

It has a fish tail.
It slides on its belly.
It lives at the bottom.
It does not belong here.
It will lead you to death.